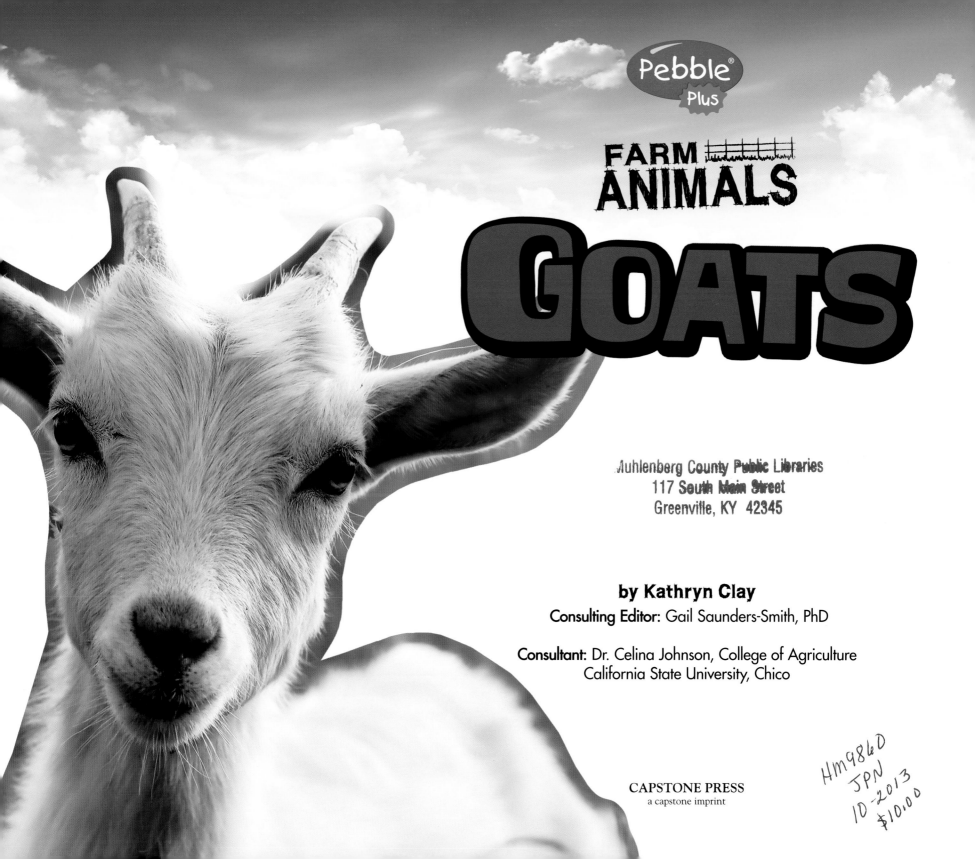

Pebble® Plus

FARM ANIMALS

GOATS

by **Kathryn Clay**

Consulting Editor: Gail Saunders-Smith, PhD

Consultant: Dr. Celina Johnson, College of Agriculture
California State University, Chico

CAPSTONE PRESS
a capstone imprint

Pebble Plus is published by Capstone Press,
1710 Roe Crest Drive, North Mankato, Minnesota 56003.
www.capstonepub.com

Library of Congress Cataloging-in-Publication Data
Clay, Kathryn.
Goats / by Kathryn Clay.
p. cm.—(Pebble plus. Farm animals)
Includes bibliographical references and index.
Summary: "Simple text and full-color photographs provide a brief introduction to goats"—Provided by publisher.
ISBN 978-1-4296-8649-5 (library binding)
ISBN 978-1-62065-301-2 (ebook PDF)
1. Goats—Juvenile literature. I. Title.
SF383.35.C53 2013
599.64'8—dc23   2011049978

Editorial Credits

Erika L. Shores, editor; Ashlee Suker, designer; Marcie Spence, media researcher; Eric Manske, production specialist

Photo Credits

Alamy: Junior Bildarchiv, 13; Ardea: John Daniels, 5; iStockphoto: BreatheFitness, 21, RonBaily, 15; Shutterstock:
Andrushchenko Dmytro, 19, Anton Balazh, 11, Dmitrijs Bindemanis, cover, 1, Ignite Lab, 17, Mircea Bezergheanu, 7,
Peter Baxter, 9

Note to Parents and Teachers

The Farm Animals series supports national science standards related to life science. This book
describes and illustrates goats. The images support early readers in understanding the text. The
repetition of words and phrases helps early readers learn new words. This book also introduces
early readers to subject-specific vocabulary words, which are defined in the Glossary section.
Early readers may need assistance to read some words and to use the Table of Contents,
Glossary, Read More, Internet Sites, and Index sections of the book.

Printed in the United States of America in North Mankato, Minnesota.
042012   006682CGF12

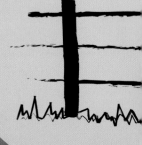

Table of Contents

Meet the Goats 4

Bucks, Does, and Kids 10

On the Farm 14

Glossary 22

Read More 23

Internet Sites 23

Index 24

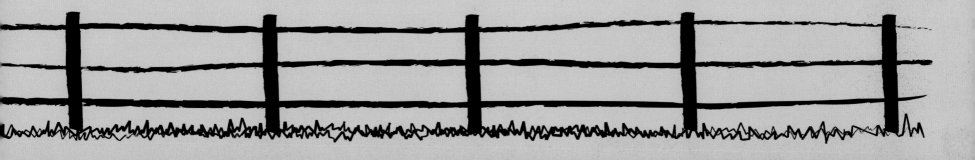

Meet the Goats

A goat's day begins early on a farm. Farmers milk goats before the sun rises.

There are about 200 breeds of goats.

Some breeds have long ears.

Others have short ears.

Goats are black, brown, gray,

red, white, or a mix of colors.

Goats are about 3 feet
(1 meter) tall.
Most goats weigh about
120 pounds (54 kilograms).

Bucks, Does, and Kids

Male goats are called bucks.

Female goats are does.

Only female goats make milk.

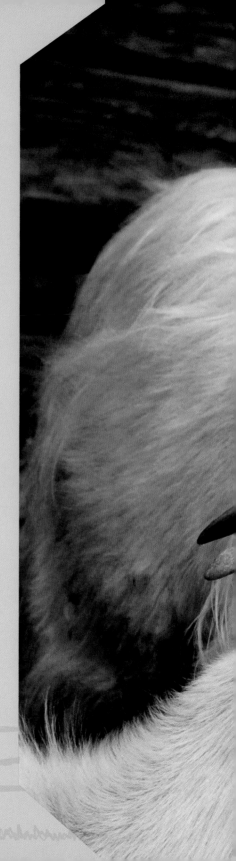

Young goats are called kids.

Two to four kids are born

at one time. Most goats live

10 to 12 years.

On the Farm

Farmers raise goats for milk and meat. Does are milked two times each day. Cheese, chocolate, and soap are made with goat milk.

Angora goats are raised
for their thick hair.
The hair is used to make
warm clothing.

Goat herds rest in pastures during warm weather. They sleep in barns when the weather is cold or rainy.

Playful goats climb on logs.

They swim in ponds.

Goats are at home on the farm.

Glossary

breed—a certain kind of animal within an animal group

buck—an adult male goat

doe—an adult female goat

herd—a group of goats

kid—a young goat

pasture—land where farm animals eat grass and exercise

Read More

Green, Emily K. *Goats.* Farm Animals. Minneapolis: Bellwether Media, 2007.

Macken, JoAnn Early. *Goats.* Animals That Live on the Farm. Pleasantville, N.Y.: Weekly Reader Pub., 2010.

Morgan, Sally. *Goats.* Down on the Farm. Laguna Hills, Calif.: QEB Pub., 2007.

Internet Sites

FactHound offers a safe, fun way to find Internet sites related to this book. All of the sites on FactHound have been researched by our staff.

Here's all you do:

Visit *www.facthound.com*

Type in this code: 9781429686495

Index

Angora goats, 16

barns, 18

bucks, 10

climbing, 20

colors, 6

does, 10

ears, 6

hair, 16

kids, 12

life span, 12

meat, 14

milk, 4, 10, 14

pastures, 18

size, 8

swimming, 20

Word Count: 168
Grade: 1
Early-Intervention Level: 15